THE LIBRARY OF
AMERICAN
LIVES AND TIMES™

DAVY
CROCKETT

The Legend
of the Wild Frontier

Richard Bruce Winders

The Rosen Publishing Group's
PowerPlus Books™
New York

This book is dedicated to my maternal grandparents: William Roscoe Bourne, "A Son of Old Kentucky" and Halene Alice Buffington Bourne, my first history teacher.

Published in 2003 by The Rosen Publishing Group, Inc.
29 East 21st Street, New York, NY 10010

First Edition

Editor's Note: All quotations have been reproduced as they appeared in the letters and diaries from which they were borrowed. No correction was made to the inconsistent spelling that was common in that time period.

Library of Congress Cataloging-in-Publication Data

Winders, Richard Bruce, 1953–
Davy Crockett: the legend of the wild frontier / Richard Bruce Winders.
   p. cm. — (The library of American lives and times)
Includes bibliographical references (p.) and index.
ISBN 0-8239-5747-0 (library binding)
1. Crockett, Davy, 1786–1836—Juvenile literature. 2. Pioneers—Tennessee—Biography—Juvenile literature. 3. Frontier and pioneer life—Tennessee—Juvenile literature. 4. Tennessee—Biography—Juvenile literature. 5. Legislators—United States—Biography—Juvenile literature. 6. United States. Congress. House—Biography—Juvenile literature. [1. Crockett, Davy, 1786–1836. 2. Pioneers. 3. Legislators.] I. Title. II. Series.
F436.C95 W56 2003
976.8'04'092—dc21

                            2001006174

Manufactured in the United States of America

CONTENTS

Preface: Meet a Frontier Legend

From the *Davy Crockett Almanack* (1835):

> *After the fuss the public have made about an individual of my humble pretensions, and the mighty deal of attention and good cheer I have received in all sections of the country, where I have been ahead, my heart has swelled as big as a Bison's, with pure gratitude. To repay all this, I mean to amuse them with some of my adventures with the wild varmints and colts of the West, and with adventures of the backwoodsman generally. Owing to the partiality of my fellow citizens, I have been made a Congressman, am from home (at Washington) half the year; but should any of my readers find me "at home," on the Big Clover Creek, Tennessee, they shall be treated with a good*

This portrait of David Crockett was painted by James H. Shegogue in 1831. Crockett was an American frontier hero, pioneer, and politician. He used humor and exaggerated images of himself as a soldier and a hunter to gain admiration and to rise to political positions.

This woodcut appeared in the 1837 *Davy Crockett Almanack*. The yearly publication told stories of his adventures as a frontiersman and hunter, which helped to spread his fame.

raccoon pie, and bush eels fried in butter—which are dishes my wife cooks to perfection. They shall have the softest white-oak log to sit on, and the best bearskin to sleep on, which my house affords. I will take them out on a coon hunt, show 'em how to tree a wildcat, and take a blizzard at a bear. They can take a walk in my crab-apple orchard, and see the alligator pear trees. And as a matter-of-fact, I will convince them that I can run faster, jump higher, squat lower, dive deeper, stay under longer, and come up drier, than any man in the whole county.

1. Crockett's Early Years

For much of American history, the name David Crockett has held a certain fascination for people of all ages. Who would not be interested in a man reported to be half horse and half alligator—a man who ran faster, jumped higher, and dove deeper than did any person alive? As one popular song later claimed, he had "killed him a bear when he was only three." Certainly these are feats for the record book.

David Crockett, or Davy, as he is fondly known today, is a frontier legend. As with all legends, though, some facts about his life have been exaggerated. Others have been entirely made up. After all, legends are by nature bigger than life. Something about legendary men and women sets them apart from most other people, something that makes them special. Historians have worked to sort through the many Crockett legends to discover the truth about this beloved figure.

Born in eastern Tennessee in 1786, David grew up, as did so many young men like him, in a land that was still a wilderness. Skills other than those gained from books

David Crockett was born near present-day Rogersville, Tennessee. This is a picture of his birthplace. The building has been preserved as a historic site by the State of Tennessee Department of Environment and Conservation.

were the most valuable. Marksmanship and wrestling were more than just games, because war could erupt between the frontiersmen and their Native American neighbors at any time. A frontiersman had to be a farmer, a hunter, and a businessman if he was to take care of himself and his family. David excelled at the first two professions. The last one always gave him trouble.

The America that David Crockett lived in was very different from today's America. The Declaration of Independence was only ten years old in 1786, when

David Crockett was born. The United States had a population of less than 4 million, compared to today's more than 280 million. In 1786, the United States was made up of only thirteen states, which had all been colonies of Britain. These states were located along the Atlantic coast and situated east of the Appalachian Mountains. The U.S. Constitution, which outlined the legal framework for the new nation, would not be adopted for another three years.

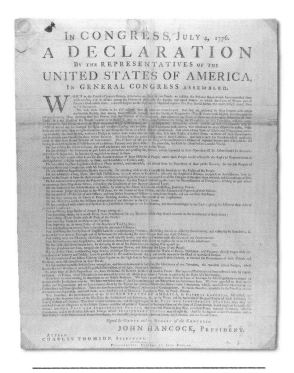

The thirteen American colonies used the Declaration of Independence to proclaim their independence from Great Britain. They adopted this document on July 4, 1776.

Crockett's ancestors were French Protestants, or Huguenots, who were driven from France by an intolerant Catholic king, Louis XIV. The Crocketts settled in Ireland, where they intermarried with English and Irish folk. Ireland was a poor land where little opportunity existed to make a good living. Around 1708, Joseph Louis Crockett and his wife, Sarah Stewart, crossed the Atlantic Ocean, bound for a new world and what they hoped would be a better future. They settled in New York

Henri Abraham Chatelain created this map of Ireland in about 1705.
David Crockett's ancestors fled to the north of Ireland in 1672
after experiencing religious persecution in France.

and began to raise their family. Joseph was the great-grandfather of the legendary David Crockett.

Early Americans were a restless people. A pattern of movement among them emerged that would be repeated throughout the nation's early history. The Crocketts participated in this great migration in the eighteenth century. They made their way southward, traveling through the green valleys that led to Pennsylvania, Virginia, and North Carolina. Following the course of a valley was much easier than crossing over hills and mountains. The valley made a natural pathway for the frontiersmen.

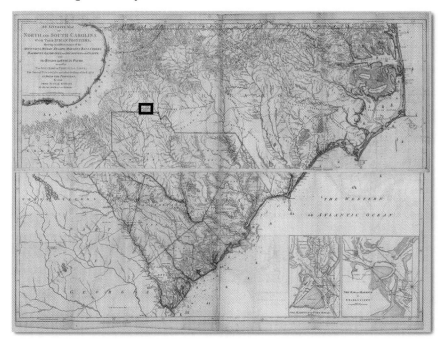

Henry Mouzon and others made this map of North Carolina and South Carolina, based on a William Faden 1777 atlas. Kings Mountain is outlined in blue. David Crockett's father fought the British for America's independence at Kings Mountain in North Carolina.

Joseph Louis Crockett's son David, the first Crockett to be named David, arrived in the backcountry of what today is called North Carolina with his family around 1776. A short time later, he and his wife were killed by Native Americans who were angry at settlers for moving into the area. The Crocketts' death highlighted the challenges of living in a region where danger never was far away. David's sons, John, Joseph, and James, stayed in North Carolina to make their own way in life.

John, who would father the legendary David Crockett, married Rebecca Hawkins sometime around 1780. John and Rebecca had a large family of six sons and three daughters. Large families were not uncommon on the frontier. David Crockett, their fifth son, was born on August 17, 1786, in eastern Tennessee. Named for his grandfather, David was destined for fame, if not for fortune.

John Crockett owned and operated a tavern to provide for his wife and children. In the past, taverns were more than just places to stop for a drink with friends. They played a vital role in politics, commerce, and travel. The owner and his family usually lived at the tavern. Travelers could stop at the tavern for food and lodging. Local residents in the vicinity of the tavern often gathered there on days when court was in session to learn the latest news. Taverns were important places, and their owners were important people. Besides running a tavern, John Crockett served for a

This photograph shows Chisholm Tavern, which was completed in 1792 in Knox County, Tennessee. One of the landmarks of eastern Tennessee, this tavern probably resembles the one operated by John Crockett around that time.

time as a local judge, hearing court cases that came before him.

Tennessee was not yet a state when David Crockett was born there. The region had been a part of North Carolina during colonial times, something that continued after North Carolina became a state in 1789. After the formation of the United States, the former colonies agreed to give up their claims to their western territories. This was in exchange for the national government's help in paying the debts the states had acquired during

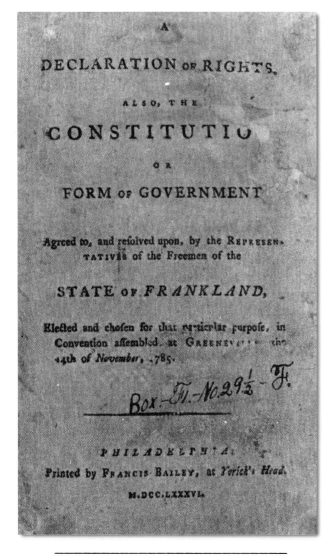

In January 1785, Frankland, also called Franklin, adopted a declaration of rights. In 1796, however, the area became part of Tennessee.

the war for independence from Britain, called the American Revolution. Though Tennessee was still a part of North Carolina, the inhabitants there felt separated from their governing officials to the east. They believed that it was time to govern themselves. The people living in Tennessee voted to form a new state, which they named Frankland. They even went so far as to elect their own officials. Later, Frankland became known as Franklin. North Carolina and the government of the United States refused to recognize the actions of Franklin's inhabitants. Support for Franklin collapsed as communication with the East improved and plans developed for formal statehood. In

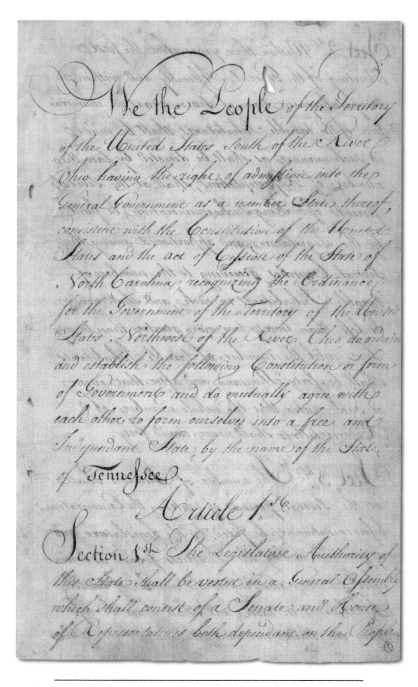

The terms of Tennessee's first constitution were made public in 1796. The Constitution was sent to Philadelphia that year as part of Tennessee's application for statehood.

1796, Tennessee officially joined the Union. At that time, Franklin's government dissolved and the region became part of the new state of Tennessee. Years of self-reliance among Tennessee's citizens had made them fiercely independent and unafraid to fight for their rights.

Commerce helped to fuel the young state's economy. Tennessee was linked with the eastern states by a network of dirt-road highways that snaked through the mountain passes to Virginia and North Carolina. John Crockett's tavern was located on the road that led from the eastern Tennessee community of Knoxville to the towns of western Virginia. As the people of the West struggled to do business with the people across the mountains to the east, these small roads became more important and more heavily traveled. Young David saw men drive herds of hogs and cattle on their way to markets in Virginia and Maryland. He also saw eastern merchants travel these roads with packhorses, carts, and wagons filled with manufactured goods destined for sale in the small towns that were springing up farther west.

Life on the frontier was difficult for settlers. John Crockett had to struggle to support his family, despite the income he earned from operating a tavern. When David was about eight, John Crockett built a mill along Cove Creek. As taverns were, mills were important businesses in frontier communities. Powered by running water, the machinery of the mill turned large stones that ground

This Conestoga-style Tennessee wagon from the 1800s is part of a frontier travel exhibit at the Tennessee State Museum. The wagon, which resembles a flatboat on wheels, was used to transport quantities of goods along primitive roads.

grain into flour. The energy of the water could also be used to drive saws for cutting lumber needed for building. However, owning a mill was a risky business because the same stream that powered it could bring destruction during floods. One such flood washed away John Crockett's mill and left him deep in debt. Thus, the Crockett family was always in need of money and never seemed able to get ahead.

John Crockett found himself unsuccessful in other business ventures, too. He purchased several pieces of

John Crockett built a grist mill in Lawrence County, Tennessee, in 1821. A year later his grist mill, a machine for grinding grain, was washed away by a flood. This replica of the mill is on display at the David Crockett State Park Museum in Tennessee.

land, probably hoping, as did other frontiersmen, that these could be sold for a profit to newcomers to the area. The U.S. government allowed settlers to buy land on credit, a way to make it easier for people without money to own property. However, many frontiersmen were unable to make the final payments on their land purchases. Crockett's father lost his land and his tavern when he was unable to pay his creditors. It appears that the new owner of the tavern allowed the Crockett family to stay on and operate the tavern.

Boys grew up fast on the frontier. They had plenty of time to play and explore, but boys were also expected to work around the home. Responsibilities increased with age. When David was about twelve years old, his father sent him on his first adventure away from home. A man named Jacob Siler was driving a herd of cattle from eastern Tennessee to Virginia and needed someone to help him. John Crockett agreed to hire out David as Siler's assistant. David, who had little choice in the matter, packed his spare clothing and left with Siler. The trip, although it offered the young boy new scenery, was uneventful. They covered the 250 miles (402 km) with little trouble.

David was eager to return home, but Siler had other plans for him. He liked David because he was a hard worker and a good companion. David did not want to hurt the man's feelings and could not say no when Siler asked him to stay on and live with Siler and his family in Virginia. David also feared that his father would be angry if he refused to stay with Siler, because the Crocketts needed the money that David might earn from Siler. The boy hid his disappointment and pretended to be pleased to become the newest member of the Siler household.

Then fortune came David's way. One Sunday afternoon, after he had spent nearly a month with the Silers, he met a wagoner, or a man who drove a freight wagon, who had often stopped at his father's tavern. He explained his situation to the man and asked for help in returning to his family. The wagoner told David that he and his sons were going to spend the night at a tavern 7 miles (11 km) down the road. If David could get there by morning, he would give him a ride back to Tennessee.

David returned to the Siler house and acted as if all was well. He gathered his belongings, placed in his pocket the money he had earned from working for Siler, and waited for the family to go to sleep. Finally, with just a few hours left until sunrise, David slipped out of the house, ready to escape from his gentle but unwanted captivity. He left the Siler house without saying farewell, because he did not want to hurt their feelings. He was also afraid they would try to convince him to stay.

The walk to meet his rescuers was difficult. Not only did David have to travel for miles (km) through the dark woods without a light, but it was snowing heavily. Relying on the tracking skills he had learned while growing up on the frontier, David reached the wagoner's camp at the tavern before sunrise. The snow had been cold and wet, but David knew that it covered his tracks, preventing Siler from knowing where he had gone. True to his word, the wagoner helped David return home. His family was glad to have him back.

John Crockett soon decided that it was time for his younger sons, by then almost in their teens, to attend a neighborhood school run by Benjamin Kitchen. Although David left little description of the school in his later writings, it was probably like other frontier schools. Education of children on the frontier was a responsibility mostly left to their families. Parents who could afford tutors hired them to instruct the children. Some of the more educated tutors offered advanced subjects, such as Greek, Latin, French, geography, and history. Frontier schools, however, taught only the basic subjects known as the three R's; reading, writing, and arithmetic. Often these schools were run by men who traveled from community to community. When a traveling scholar found a town with no school, he rented a vacant building and enrolled students for a fee. Often the fee was paid with corn, bacon, or firewood instead of with money, but the teacher usually received enough in trade to care for himself. Schools were seasonal, closing down during planting and harvesting times because the students were needed at home to help in the fields. By today's standards, frontier schools were primitive. Despite the lack of a formal classroom setting, schools provided a valuable service.

David Crockett's experience at Mr. Kitchen's school proved short-lived, lasting for only four days. David exhibited a streak of independence that was common among frontier lads. He had already been on his own and was not keen on the idea of having to attend school. When he and an older boy had an argument at school, David waited until the end of the day and then beat up his opponent on the way home. The next day, and for several days after the incident, David pretended to set off to school each morning, but, instead of going, he hid in the woods. He believed that Mr. Kitchen would punish him for the fight. His brothers agreed to keep his secret from their father, who, they knew, would be angry.

The plan worked until Mr. Kitchen sent a note to John Crockett asking why his son had not been attending school. David was really in a fix then. His father, who could give harsh punishments, threatened to beat his truant son with a hickory stick if he did not go back to school. Wanting to escape his father's anger, David hid from him and resolved to run away from home. Young David Crockett was about to leave home for a second time, but this time it was his own choice.

2. Life on the Frontier

Young Crockett spent the next two years on his own. He was first hired on as a drover, a type of cowboy, to help move a herd of cattle to Virginia, something he already had had experience doing for Mr. Siler. His break from home was not complete at first, because one of his older brothers worked as a drover for the brother of David's boss. Once the cattle were sold, however, David told his brother that he was not going to return home with him. David was hired on as a wagoner's helper. He traveled throughout Virginia and Maryland hauling freight, such as barrels of flour. At Baltimore, a busy seaport, he wanted to widen his travels by signing on as a crewman with a ship bound for London, but his employer refused to let him go. How different David's life might have turned out had he gone to sea and not returned home to Tennessee!

It was now 1802, and he decided that it was time to head back west. He left because his employer threatened to beat him and treated him like a servant. David set off, asking for and receiving help from wagoners he encountered along the way.

This oil painting was made by George Caleb Bingham in 1850. Like many young men who grew up along the river, young David Crockett sailed up and down rivers for both work and fun. Crockett used to tell people of a childhood incident in which he and his brothers, as children, almost got swept over a waterfall while sailing in a canoe.

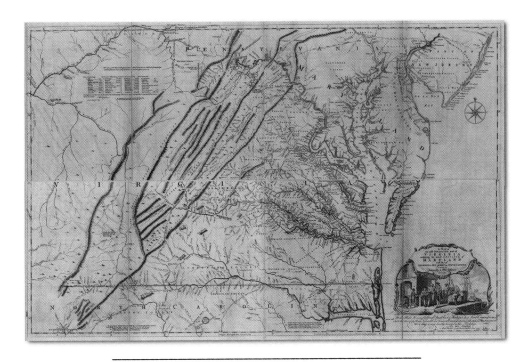

Joshua Fry and Peter Jefferson drew this 1775 map of the most inhabited part of Virginia. The map contains the whole province of Maryland, with part of Pennsylvania, New Jersey, and North Carolina. As a teenager David Crockett spent two years in Virginia working for farmers and wagoners.

One evening he reached the tavern where his family worked and lived. David Crockett, now about fifteen years old, had changed during his two-year-long adventure. He entered the tavern but did not immediately announce his return. He was unsure of how his father would react. Was he still angry that David had run away? While seated for dinner with the rest of the guests, David was finally recognized by a sister. His parents, brothers, and sisters were overjoyed to have David return home safely. He realized that his behavior had caused his family to suffer, all because he had been too proud to take responsibility for his actions.

David Crockett had left home a boy and had returned a young man. He resolved to support himself and to do what he could to help his family out of debt. He agreed to his father's request that he pay off one of the family's debts by working for six months for a creditor. He returned home after fulfilling the obligation and gave his father a receipt showing the debt had been paid. Then, without his family's knowledge, David arranged to pay off another of his father's debts by working an additional six-month term for a different creditor, a man named John Kennedy. He took pleasure in presenting the receipt to his father, who believed that his son had been sent by the creditor to collect the debt from John. David proudly explained that he had worked to pay the debt for his father and presented him the note as a present. After a year's labor, David had satisfied two of his father's creditors. He set about preparing for his own future.

Spanish money was made legal currency in the United States in 1793. The hole at the top of this coin let its owner sew or pin the money to his clothing to avoid losing it. Crockett might have handled money that looked like this.

David Crockett returned to John Kennedy and arranged to continue his employment. Kennedy, whom David described as an "old Quaker," liked young David and agreed to help him prepare himself for life on his own. Clothes were David's immediate need, but he soon found himself wanting something more. He had fallen in love with a girl who was visiting from North Carolina, and he wanted to marry her. She rejected him, however. David thought that maybe she did not want him because he lacked an education. Although he was approaching his late teens, David did not yet know how to read or write. He believed that acquiring some education would make him a more desirable suitor. Mr. Kennedy allowed David to attend a school run by one of Kennedy's sons who lived in the neighborhood. David attended the school four days per week for a period of six months. Years later he claimed that this was the only formal schooling he had ever had. It was during this time that he learned to read, write, and perform simple mathematical equations. On the frontier, these basic skills set him above many of his neighbors, who never received any formal education at all.

David Crockett became even more determined to find a wife. Another attempt also ended in failure when Crockett learned that his intended wife, Margaret Elder, had changed her mind and wanted to wed another man. Disappointed and brokenhearted by his two lost loves, he turned his attention to yet another local

This document, signed by David Crockett, sealed the marriage bond between him and Polly Finley on August 12, 1806. One year after Polly's death in 1815, Crockett married Elizabeth Patton, a widow with two small children.

girl, Mary Finley. Crockett affectionately called her Polly. The two soon decided to wed. After some effort, he received her parents' permission to wed their daughter. They probably knew that the headstrong Crockett was determined to take Polly as his wife, with or without their consent. The ceremony took place on August 16, 1806, at the Finley home. David Crockett, the son of a poor tavern keeper, with no property of his own, now had a wife to look after.

Marrying at a young age was not uncommon on the frontier. Marriage by the age of twenty-one was considered normal, because children in their late teens were expected to leave home and to make their own way in the world. The Crocketts began their married life on a small piece of rented land, where they raised corn and cattle. The Finleys had given their daughter and son-in-law two cows and two calves. Crockett was grateful for the gift, although it was not much of a start. His friend Mr. Kennedy gave the couple $15 of credit at a local store, to be used in furnishing their small cabin. David and Polly struggled hard to make ends meet. By 1809, he and his wife had two sons, John Wesley and William.

Both David and Polly excelled in the frontier skills needed for survival. Polly was an accomplished spinner, operating her spinning wheel by the fireplace in their cabin. Spinning linen thread from the flax plant was extremely important on the frontier, because families produced their own clothing. Coarse fabric woven from

Frontier women, like Polly Crockett, often became accomplished spinners. This picture of a woman operating a spinning wheel appeared in an 1807 publication, *The Book of Trades or Library of the Useful Arts.*

the homemade thread was used to make pants, shirts, coats, and dresses. Home spinning and weaving satisfied a basic need for frontier families. These basic skills were so important that they were passed on from generation to generation, as mothers taught daughters the art of turning plant fibers into cloth.

On the frontier, where money was in short supply, men could still try to earn a living by tracking and killing bears, raccoons, and other fur-bearing animals. David Crockett, who had spent most of his life in the east Tennessee woods, had become an exceptional hunter. Not only did this skill supply his family's table with fresh game, but the furs, pelts, and hides of the animals he shot could be traded to local merchants for goods.

The main tool of the frontier hunter was the long rifle. Crockett had many during his lifetime. He probably acquired his first when he worked for Mr. Kennedy. Even though he might not have owned his own rifle until he left home, he undoubtedly had already gained experience using his father's gun on childhood hunts. Frontier boys were taught to load and to fire their family's weapons at an early age to help defend the family from wild animals and Native Americans, as well as to provide food for the stew pot. The rifle, the shot bag, and the powder horn were familiar household items that could save a frontiersman and his family from enemies and starvation.

Hunters, such as David Crockett, often hung the skins of animals they had killed on the wall.

Frontier social gatherings gave men the opportunity to display their skill with rifles. Shooting matches,

This 1814 rifle, on display at the Alamo Museum, once belonged to David Crockett. Historians acknowledge that Crockett was a frequent hunter. He reportedly shot and killed 105 black bears in the fall and winter of 1825, including 17 in a single week.

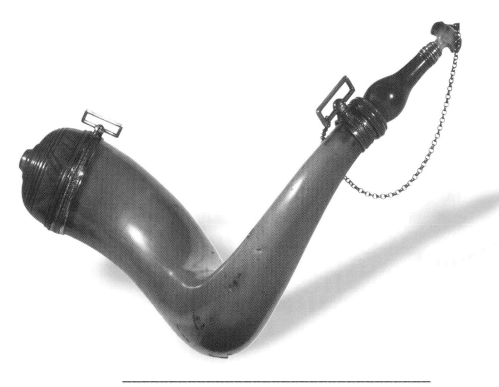

This powder horn, which belonged to David Crockett, is on display at the Tennessee State Museum. A powder horn was used to carry gunpowder and often was made from the horn of an ox or a cow.

which were a form of frontier entertainment, allowed men such as Crockett to compete for prizes. Winners often received a share of freshly slaughtered beef or a turkey instead of a cash award. One popular contest was to see whose shot could drive a nail into a board by hitting the nail squarely on its head. According to written accounts left by spectators, these contests were often very close because so many of the frontiersmen were excellent marksmen. The contest could continue even after dark. In one nighttime event, contestants fired at a candle. The object was not to hit the candle but to snuff out the flame without cutting the wick. The contest mimicked hunting small game at night by torchlight, when the flame of a torch caused animals' eyes to shine in the darkness. The first-place winner at shooting matches usually received the right to collect the used lead bullets from the target as an added bonus, to melt and recast them into new rifle balls. Crockett regularly attended these shooting events and soon earned a reputation as a crack shot.

After Crockett began his political career, he received gifts from supporters, including this silver hatchet from the Young Men of
Philadelphia. The hatchet, given to Crockett in 1835, was inscribed
with the encouraging words "Go Ahead Crockett."

3. On the Battlefield

Crockett and other frontier riflemen faced another, more serious challenge: war. A major cause of the conflict reached back to the end of the American Revolution. The British, having lost to the Americans, had agreed to abandon forts they had occupied west of the Appalachian Mountains. Although they finally left, they did not go far. British agents in Canada maintained their influence over the Native Americans in the Great Lakes regions and the Ohio Valley through trade. British agents, using Spanish Florida as a base, also had contact with Native Americans who lived south of the Ohio River. Europeans had long used Native American allies in their wars in North America. The British, who still wanted to reclaim their lost colonies, planned to use their Native American allies against the American settlers.

This is a 1755 map of Canada by Jacques-Nicolas Bellin. American settlers resented the British presence in Canada in the mid to late 1700s. The Americans worried that the British would influence the Native Americans in Canada to fight against the Americans in future conflicts.

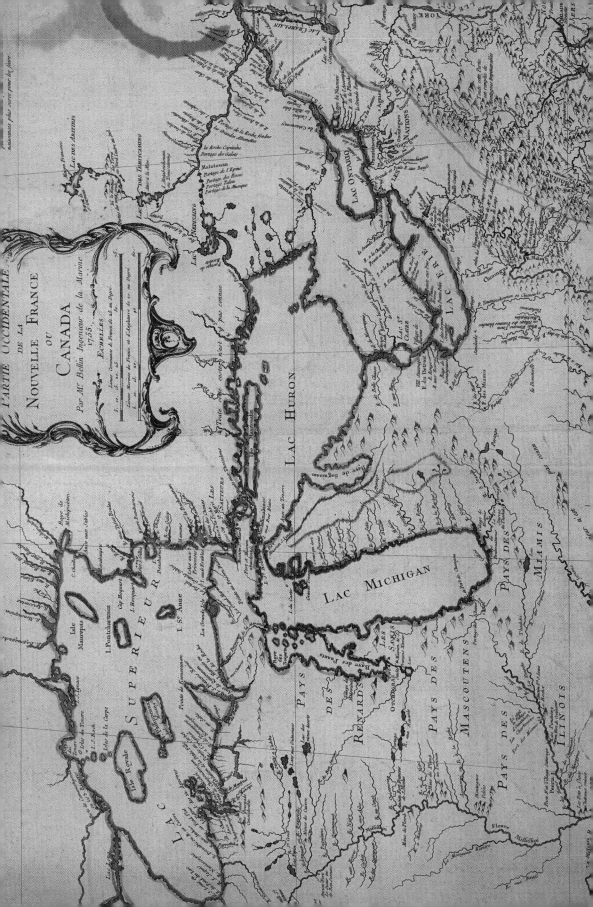

PARTIE OCCIDENTALE
DE LA
NOUVELLE FRANCE
OU
CANADA
Par Mr Bellin Ingenieur de la Marine
1755.

LAC ONTARIO

LAC ERIE

LAC HURON

LAC MICHIGAN

LAC SUPERIEUR

Isle Royale

Isle Maurepas

PAYS DES MIAMIS

PAYS DES MASCOUTENS

PAYS DES ILINOIS

PAYS DES RENARDS

Fleuve Missisipi

BATTLE OF NEW ORLEANS
AND DEATH OF MAJOR GENERAL PACKENHAM
On the 8th of January 1815.

In 1817, William Edward West painted this depiction of the Battle of New Orleans. American troops defeated the British, who attacked New Orleans on January 8, 1815.

Anger over British interference in America's affairs united Americans in what was described at the time as the Second War for Independence. In 1812, after years of growing hostility against its former colonial master, the United States declared war on Great Britain. Westerners supported the war because it offered an opportunity to end the threat on the frontier posed by Native Americans who were loyal to the British. Easterners supported the war because the British navy had disrupted trade with other nations by seizing

American ships and sailors on the open seas. The fighting at the war's outbreak took place along the U.S.-Canadian border. Soon it spread to the southern frontier where Crockett lived.

Many Native Americans living in the Old Southwest, which included Virginia, the Carolinas, Tennessee, and Kentucky, sided with the British. One powerful tribe, called the Creeks, divided into two factions. The Peace Party did not want war with the settlers. The War Party, known as the Red Sticks because they used red-colored clubs to signify war, wanted to drive the Americans from the natives' ancestral homeland. On August 30, 1813, the Red Sticks attacked and destroyed Fort Mims in southern Alabama in retaliation for an earlier attack on a band of pro-war Creeks. They burned the fort and killed nearly five hundred soldiers and settlers. The attack on Fort Mims marked the official start of the Creek War, a regional conflict within the larger, ongoing War of 1812.

The U.S. Army was not really prepared for full-scale war. The nation maintained only a small force of full-time soldiers for its defense. These men were already needed to man the forts that guarded the U.S.-Canadian border and major U.S. harbors. Each state had its own army, called a militia. The members of the militias were farmers, shopkeepers, lawyers, and other average citizens of the state. The governor could order out the militia in response to emergencies, an act taken

The Fort Mims massacre is shown in this 1874 illustration.
On August 30, 1813, Creek Indians raided this Alabama fort,
killing five hundred whites, to avenge a recent American ambush
and to recover Native American lands taken by the whites.

by Tennessee's chief executive. In this way, General
Andrew Jackson and several thousand Tennesseans,
David Crockett among them, took to the field to wage
war against the Red Sticks.

The members of the militia were only required to
serve a ninety-day enlistment before being allowed to
return home. This was a serious problem for commanders
because it took time to train an army and to prepare it for
a campaign. Crockett, because of his reputation as an
excellent woodsman, was assigned to a company of

scouts. He and his companions went ahead of the Army to locate the villages and the camps of the pro-war Creeks. In November 1813, the Tennesseans attacked and destroyed the Creek town of Tallussahatchee. Nearly all residents of the Red Stick stronghold, approximately two hundred men, women, and children, were killed or captured in the fight by the angry Tennesseans. The massacre at Fort Mims had been paid back by a bloody massacre at Tallussahatchee.

Crockett's enlistment soon expired. To Polly's disappointment, he quickly volunteered to serve another term in the militia. After supplying his family with enough

The Battle of Tallussahatchee, pictured here in an engraving by Devereaux that likely dates from the 1850s, took place on November 3, 1813. General John Coffee led Tennessee volunteers, including Crockett, in an attack on the Creek village. The Americans killed all adult male Creeks and captured Creek women and children.

"Battling the Creek Indians at Tallussahatchee"
from *A Narrative of the Life of David Crockett,*
Written by Himself

We took them all prisoners that came
out to us in this way; but I saw some
warriors run into a house, until I counted
forty-six of them. We pursued them until
we got near the house, when we saw
a squaw sitting in the door,
and she placed her feet against the bow
she had in her hand, and then took an
arrow, and, raising her feet, she drew
with all her might, and let fly at us,
and she killed a man, whose name,
I believe, was Moore. He was a lieutenant,
and his death so enraged us all, that she was
fired on. . . .

meat and firewood to see them through the winter, he returned to the field. He was not with General Jackson and the main army when they attacked and defeated the Red Sticks at the Battle of Horseshoe Bend in Alabama on March 27–28, 1814. Soon after their defeat at Horseshoe Bend, the pro-war Creeks agreed to sign a peace treaty. Crockett resumed his duties as a scout and was promoted to the rank of third sergeant. For all purposes, however, the Creek War was finished. Although Crockett had signed on for a third enlistment, he hired a substitute to finish his last term and returned home to Polly.

4. Building a Reputation

David, Polly, and their two sons were living in Franklin County, Tennessee, in 1815. They had moved there before the outbreak of the war. Crockett had been away from home off and on for more than a year, and it was time to get back to being a husband and a father. That summer Polly gave birth to a daughter named Margaret. The Crockett household had grown to five. Sadly for the family, though, Polly died just weeks after Margaret's birth. Crockett, now a widower, had three children to care for by himself.

Death on the frontier, although sad, was an ever-present fact of life. Wild animals, frontier warfare, and accidents took a heavy toll on settlers. Disease also struck down countless men, women, and children. With death in its many forms all around them, people on the frontier accepted the passing of loved ones and moved on with their own lives as best they could.

The following year, Crockett took another wife to help care for his family. This was not an uncommon practice on the frontier. His new bride, Elizabeth Patton, was a

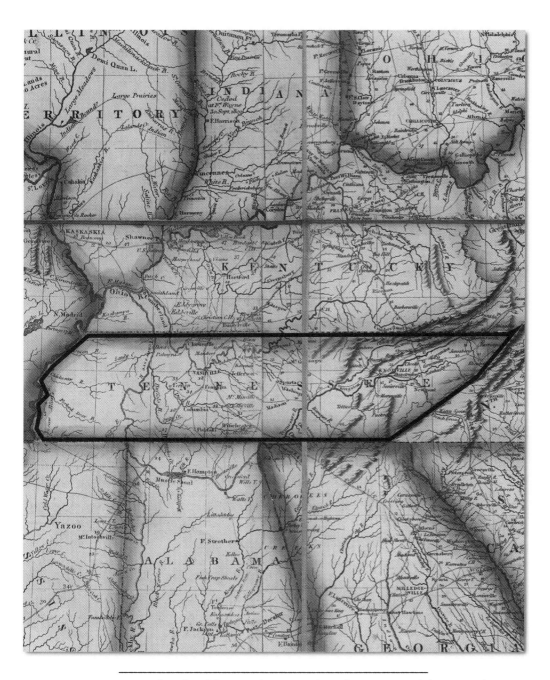

Tennessee is outlined in blue on this map that shows part of the United States and that was created around 1816 by John Melish. A few times, David Crockett moved his family from one part of Tennessee to another, hoping to improve his fortunes in business, farming, and hunting.

widow with two young children, George and Margaret Ann. Perhaps romantic feelings were involved, but the marriage had practical advantages for Crockett. He gained not only a mother for his children but also the title to her deceased husband's farm.

One way to get through a tragedy was to pick up and move. Moving was viewed as a symbolic act of leaving the past behind by reaching out for whatever promises the future might hold. Crockett and several friends set off for Alabama to explore possible new homesteads. Crockett became ill on the trip and was left behind at a stranger's cabin to get well or to die. His friends did not expect him to recover. Soon news reached Elizabeth that she was once again a widow. She was surprised one day to see Crockett emerge from the back of a wagon, pale and thin but still alive. Historians believe that he had suffered from malaria, a disease characterized by sudden spells of fever and chills such as those Crockett described as having attacked him.

By 1817, Crockett was well enough to move his family to a new home in Lawrence County, Tennessee. In some ways he followed the pattern set by his own father, John. He hoped that each move would bring him better luck. He farmed, hunted, and entered small business ventures that repeatedly failed. He built a mill but it was washed away, just as was his father's mill. Despite Elizabeth's help, he fell into debt that he could not escape. In 1822, the Crocketts moved once again, this time to western Tennessee near the Obion River. By now, Crockett had become involved in politics.

Crockett had picked the location of his family's new home the year before. Traveling with his son John Wesley and Abram Henry, a hired hand, Crockett explored the region for several weeks before selecting a clearing near one of west Tennessee's many creeks. The area had not been open very long for settlement, as the Native Americans living there had only recently signed a treaty giving up the land. Few frontiersmen had yet ventured into the tangle of trees, brush, and cane. The region had a strange appearance because an earthquake had struck nearby in 1811. The force of the quake was so strong that it caused the Mississippi River to run backward for several days. The land sank in spots that filled with water and formed lakes. These newly formed lakes dotted west Tennessee and added to the problem of traveling through the area. Instead of being scared off by this harsh landscape, Crockett was pleased by what he found. There were few settlers with whom to compete for prime land, and game was so plentiful that the land was a hunter's paradise.

David Crockett was about to establish his reputation as a great hunter and frontiersman. Deer, elk, and other smaller game filled the woods, but bears were what he wanted. Most Americans living today do not think of dining on bear steaks, but in Crockett's time the animal was considered a wonderful food source. In

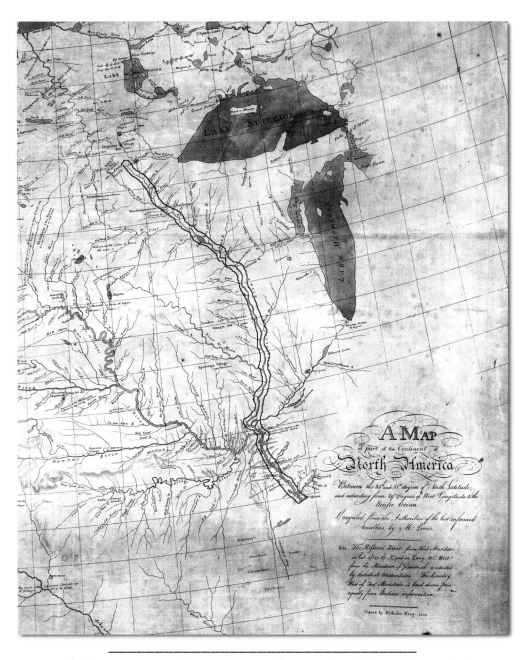

Nicholas King copied this 1805 map from a sketch by William Clark.
It shows western North America, from Lake Michigan and Lake
Superior to the Pacific Ocean, including southern Canada and
northern Mexico. The Mississippi River is circled in red.

addition to the meat, bearskins brought a high price at market. Bear fat was turned into grease and was used in many frontier homes as a lubricant and a medicine. Bear fat and other animal fats could even be used to make candles to light the otherwise dimly lit cabins. Frontiersmen had several reasons to think of bears as valuable game.

Hunting bears became almost a full-time job for Crockett. Bears were hunted with hounds that tracked animals by smell. The dogs would be taken through the woods until they caught a bear's scent. The hunters then turned the hounds loose to chase the bear. The hunters followed behind and listened to the sounds of the barking

"Crockett on a Hunt"
from *Sketches and Eccentricities of Col. David Crockett, of West Tennessee*

I sounded my horn, and dogs come howling 'bout me, ready for a chase. Old Ratler was a little lame—a bear bit him on the shoulder; but Soundwell, Tiger, and the rest of them were mighty anxious. . . . I leaned old Betsy 'gin a tree, and laid down. I s'pose I had been lying there nearly an hour, when I heard old Tiger open. He opened once or twice, and old Ratler gave a long howl; the balance joined in and I knew the elk were up. I jumped up and seized my rifle. I could hear nothing but one continuous roar of all my dogs, coming right towards me. Though I was an old hunter, the music made my hair stand on end.

dogs in the distance. When approached by the hounds, a bear might fight the dogs or climb a tree to try to escape. The hunters could tell when either occurred by the sounds of the dogs' barking. Catching up with their hounds, the hunters would shoot the bear, skin it, and cut the carcass into pieces. Packhorses were usually brought up, if the woods were not too dense, to help carry the load home. Although this might sound like an easy process, it took skill to know the areas in which bears would likely be found. A person also had to have courage to set off into the wilderness to hunt bears, because these animals are strong and can fight back fiercely when cornered.

Crockett's reputation as a hunter spread across west Tennessee. Not only did he fill his family's table with meat, he frequently shared the meat with others living in the vicinity. Crockett took great delight in telling people about his adventures hunting bears, and he said that in one season alone, he killed 105 bears. Helping rid the area of wild animals made him a local hero.

One adventure during this period nearly cost him his life. His opponent was not a bear but the mighty Mississippi River. Crockett decided that there was money to be made by harvesting the local woods for timber. He hired several men and set them to work cutting staves, or planks, used to make wooden pipes and barrels. He also had the men build two wooden flatboats on which to transport his cargo to New Orleans. Once the boats were ready, he and his crew launched

UNDER MY WINGS EVERY THING PROSPERS

John L. Bóqueta de Woiseri made this 1806 painting of New Orleans to celebrate the Louisiana Purchase, the sale of land in western America to the United States from France on April 30, 1803. Around the time of this transaction, Crockett was building his reputation as a hunter and frontiersman.

themselves in the Obion River and floated down to its junction with the Mississippi River. Although they were accomplished woodsmen, Crockett and his men had never manned or piloted flatboats. The Mississippi must have seemed like a vast ocean to them, and they found themselves at the mercy of the river. Crockett had the two boats tied together. Unable to reach the shore and stop for the night, the boats floated down the river in darkness. Near Memphis, Tennessee, the boats struck the tip of an island and began to sink. The crew was on deck when the accident occurred, but Crockett was in a small cabin on one of the flatboats. Water rushed through the door to the room, trapping him inside. He pushed his arms through a small window and attracted his men's attention. Pulling with all their might, they freed Crockett from the sinking boat, nearly skinning him as he passed through the tight opening. He and his men spent the rest of the night on the island and were picked up in the morning by a rescue party sent out from Memphis. The boats and the cargo could not be saved. Crockett lost his investment in the wreck but gained friends in Memphis who would help him with his growing political career.

5. A Political Career Is Born

In the first part of the 1800s, politics underwent important changes. Before the American Revolution, men had to own land before they could hold political office. Many positions were appointed, which meant they usually were filled by men who came from influential families. People without either property or connections had little say in making laws. Five words in the Declaration of Independence of 1776 started a real revolution in the American political system. The simple statement that "all men are created equal" placed the frontiersman on the same level as the aristocrats who lived in the East. Most states quickly abolished owning property as a requirement for either holding office or voting. The American Revolution had prompted a real democratic revolution that swept across the young nation. David Crockett and others like him benefited from these sweeping changes.

Crockett had proven himself popular with his friends and neighbors long before moving to western Tennessee. In 1814, during the Creek War, his fellow soldiers in the militia elected him to the rank of sergeant, proving that they not only liked him but also they trusted him. Two years later, he was elected lieutenant, an even higher rank. By 1818, Crockett had been elected colonel of the 57th Regiment of Tennessee Militia. Involvement in the militia was important for anyone who wanted to run for political office, because it was a way to become well known in the community. Crockett used the title of colonel for the rest of his life.

Crockett held his first civil office after the Creek War ended. When living in Lawrence Country in 1817, his neighbors elected him justice of the peace, an act

The David Crockett Courthouse in Lawrenceburg, Tennessee, was built right after Crockett left the county in 1821. It was enlarged between 1848 and 1850. This photograph was taken around 1903, about a year before the courthouse was torn down to make room for a new one.

The above signature of David Crockett was taken from an 1820 contract that he signed, making Joseph Halford a Lawrence County constable. Not until age eighteen or so did Crockett learn to read and write. As a child, he had received little formal schooling.

later confirmed by the Tennessee state legislature. His duties included settling small disagreements and helping the constable to catch and to punish more serious offenders. The following year, he was also elected commissioner of the new town of Lynchburg, a position that involved him in city government. In 1821, he ran for the legislature to represent the counties of Hickman and Lawrence and won. First colonel, then judge and town commissioner, and then a member of the state legislature, Crockett was a man of some importance in Tennessee. Colonel Crockett had become more than just a simple frontiersman.

Crockett's move to the western part of Tennessee in 1822 did not interrupt his political career. He was soon running for office in the state legislature in the newly formed district that contained his home in the Obion River bottomland. Crockett claimed that he reentered politics in 1822 as a joke. He had traveled to Jackson, a

This portrait of David Crockett in hunting clothes appeared in D.W.C. Baker's 1875 *A Texas Scrap-Book*. The portrait was based on an 1834 painting by John G. Chapman.

small town about 40 miles (64 km) from his home, with a load of hides to sell. As he was leaving Jackson, he met some friends who wanted to talk. The election was drawing closer, and one of the candidates asked Crockett why he himself did not run. He did not commit to anything but later read in a newspaper that he had been officially entered in the race. Thinking that a trick had been played on him, he decided to campaign for the office and was elected. Thus, his absence from the statehouse had been only temporary.

Crockett's style of campaigning for office followed typical frontier fashion. Before the invention of radio or

This 1848 engraving shows men in the process of house-raising. Men built many log cabins together on the American frontier. People often gathered at house-raisings to share one another's company. Politicians used such occasions to give speeches.

television, candidates had to make many public appearances for voters to get to know them. Events such as court sessions, market days, house-raising, shucking bees, militia drills, and weddings brought people together. Candidates used these gatherings to speak to the crowd. Crockett realized that entertainment was more popular with his neighbors than a discussion of serious issues would be. When his turn came to talk, he would tell humorous stories about hunting and other things that were important to the frontiersmen who came to

David Rent Etter painted this portrait of Andrew Jackson.
Jackson became the seventh president of the United States and,
in 1828, was the first westerner to be elected president.

listen. Many politicians of the time would often speak for several hours. Crockett liked to be last on the program. When introduced he would tell a few jokes and make the tired crowd laugh. Having won over the crowd quickly with his easygoing manner, Crockett would stop after several minutes and invite them all to join him at the bar for a drink, on him.

Politics in the early 1800s reflected the democratic changes that America was undergoing. Two basic ideas about government had developed after the American Revolution. In one model, the individual states kept the majority of their rights and acted almost like independent countries. They agreed to work together for the common good of all states, such as in cases of defense and trade. The other model placed more power in the hands of the national Congress, which met at Washington. In the early days of the republic, the people who believed in the first model were called Democratic-Republicans, and those in the second group were called Federalists. The party names would change, but the ideas about government stayed the same throughout the nineteenth century.

By the mid-1820s, another Tennessean, General Andrew Jackson, had gained a popular political following. Jackson had won fame at the Battle of Horseshoe Bend in 1814, when his men had defeated the pro-war Red Sticks. On January 8, 1815, Jackson became an even bigger hero when his army defeated the British at

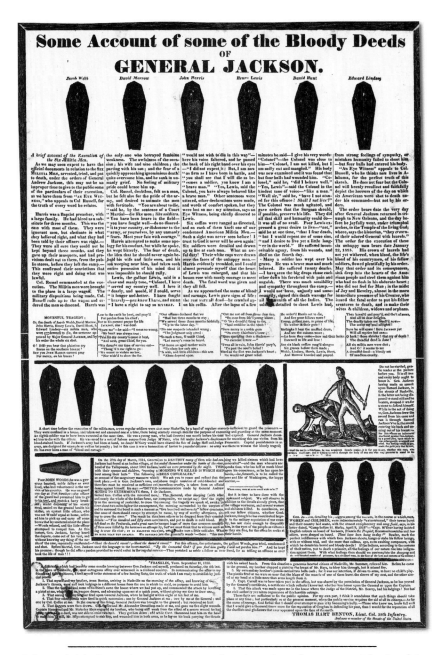

A broadside is a sheet of paper that is printed on one side. In this political broadside, articles accuse Andrew Jackson of military cruelty, and coffins are drawn to depict him as a murderous tyrant. The broadside was probably used in the 1828 presidential elections.

New Orleans during the final battle of the War of 1812. Early Americans celebrated the date of this important victory over their old enemy with the same passion they brought to celebrating the Fourth of July. Jackson, a war hero, became a nationally recognized figure. The fact that he was from Tennessee focused national attention on that state and its politics.

Jackson's ideas about government made him a champion of the common man. He complained that the hold on political office by rich and powerful men must be broken. Supporters overlooked the fact that Jackson himself was rich and powerful. They concentrated on his demand for an end to special privileges enjoyed by few men and for equal access to government by all men.

General Jackson had risen to his place in society from a poor background. His family had died in the American Revolution, and he even had been a British prisoner of war in 1781. Born on the border between North Carolina and South Carolina, he studied law as a young man and moved to Nashville when it was still a frontier community. Lawyers were needed to settle land disputes. Jackson established himself as a successful lawyer and was even appointed a judge. By the time of the War of 1812, Jackson was not only a plantation owner but a major general in the Tennessee militia as well. His victories at Horseshoe Bend and New Orleans made him famous. His success showed that even though a person started out poor, the young republic made it possible to better oneself.

This 1807 drawing by Benjamin Henry Latrobe features the north and south porticoes, or porches, that later would be added to the White House. With the finishing of the porticoes in 1829, the image of the White House as we know it today was complete.

By 1824, Jackson had enough support to run for president of the United States. Through a strange twist, he lost the election to John Quincy Adams, even though Jackson had won more votes. His supporters, who included Crockett, claimed the election had been stolen. They worked even harder to place Jackson in the White House, the official residence of the president, when the next election came around. Jackson's election in 1828 was a major victory for the frontier, because it was the first time that a man who lived west of the Appalachian Mountains had been elected president.

6. On the Campaign Trail

Crockett was already a congressman in Washington by the time President Jackson arrived in town. Several years earlier, he had decided to run for the U.S. Congress. He lost his first attempt in 1825. His flatboat wreck near Memphis, however, proved to be of use in spite of its loss of cargo. One of the residents of the city who had helped him and his crew was a prosperous businessman named Major M. B. Winchester. His new friend told him to run again for Congress and offered to help pay for his campaign and other expenses. Crockett's frontier humor and charm aided him on the campaign trail, and, in 1827, voters in western Tennessee sent him to work for them in the House of Representatives.

David Crockett claimed that he, like Jackson, stood for the common man. He delighted in pointing out the difference between the rich and powerful versus the simple people of the frontier. During one campaign, he told voters that his opponent walked on rugs woven of finer material than the dresses worn by the voters' wives. After Crockett had been elected to the Tennessee

HALL OF REPRESENTATIVES. WASH. D.C.

This 1832 watercolor by Alexander Jackson Davis shows
the Hall of Representatives in Washington, D.C. In this hall,
American politicians, such as Crockett, debated the
destiny of an expanding young nation.

legislature, another member jokingly called Crockett "the gentleman from the cane." This reference to Crockett's frontier background caused some assembly-men to laugh. Crockett later found a ruffle on the ground that had come off a man's fancy dress shirt and looked like the ruffles worn by the man who had embar-rassed him. He pinned the ruffle to the front of his homespun jacket and walked onto the floor of the legis-lature. He looked so funny that soon everyone was laughing. Crockett had used humor to turn the tables on his attacker. Thereafter he proudly used the title the Gentleman from the Cane, because it highlighted his connection with the common man.

As a member of the Tennessee legislature and the House of Representatives, Crockett supported bills that would help improve the conditions of frontiersmen and small farmers. A major concern of his was that these men and women should have a fair chance to own land. Many early settlers had moved to the frontier ahead of government land offices. They had picked out the land they liked, had built cabins, and had planted crops. Problems developed when land speculators, men who bought land hoping to sell it for a profit, purchased some of the settlers' lands from the government at the rate of

---

Next spread: George Catlin's engraving of the U.S. Military Academy at West Point, New York, published in 1828, is one of the earliest depictions of the school. Crockett claimed that the military academy gave enrollment privileges to the sons of the rich and powerful.

$1.25 per acre ($3.13/ha). Settlers who had squatted, or moved onto the land without legal ownership, would have to buy their farms from the speculator or move and start again somewhere else. Making matters worse for Crockett's neighbors in western Tennessee was the fact that the region had once belonged to North Carolina. Governmental officials there had issued land grants in western Tennessee to its citizens who had fought in the American Revolution, as payment for their military service in the war. Squatters faced a constant threat of being evicted by someone holding one of the North Carolina land grants. Congressman Crockett introduced a number of laws that would give squatters the opportunity to buy their land legally. Unfortunately, his bill was never passed.

Crockett also spoke out against the U.S. Military Academy at West Point, New York. The school had been established in 1802, to train officers for the U.S. Army. Students were selected by the various members of Congress who had the power to hand out appointments to young men in their districts. Crockett claimed that only the sons of the rich and powerful received appointments and the free college education that went along with it. Thus, this was a special privilege for the wealthy and ought to end. Crockett, who had served in the militia and had fought in a war without any special training other than that of having grown up on the frontier, also claimed that the school was a waste of

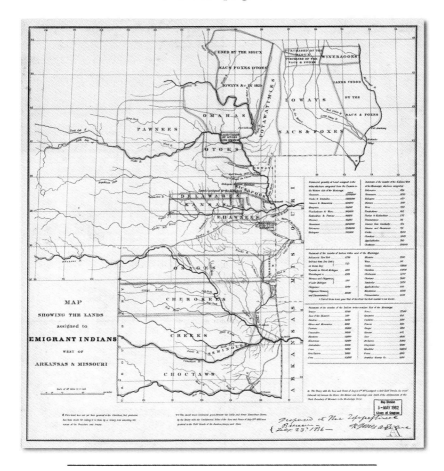

This 1836 map shows the lands assigned to Native Americans west of Arkansas and Missouri. Native Americans were forced by the U.S. government to take unsettled western prairie land in exchange for the tribes' more desirable territories.

time and tax money. The poor were obligated to pay the taxes that supported the school, he argued, but it was the rich who got to attend the exclusive academy. Although Crockett was wrong in his claim that only the sons of rich people went to West Point, his attitude reflected that held by many militia officers.

Crockett also spoke against the unfair treatment of Native Americans by the government. It might seem odd that someone whose grandparents had been killed by Native Americans, and who had fought in the Creek War against the Red Sticks, would try to help his former enemies. Crockett had come to see that these people confronted some of the same problems that others had faced living on the frontier. President Jackson supported a plan to force all Native Americans living east of the Mississippi River to move to several areas located west of the river designated as "permanent Indian Territory." Supporters of the Indian Removal Act of 1830 claimed that Anglo settlers and Native Americans could never live together in peace. The answer, they said, was to separate the two peoples. Crockett and others who opposed the plan said that removing the different groups from their ancient homelands would be cruel. They also claimed that land speculators were behind the plan to move the Native Americans off their lands, because these speculators could then buy the land from the government. Removal took place despite the objections of Crockett and other opponents.

7. Becoming Famous

Crockett's colorful behavior and outspoken support for certain unpopular causes made people take notice of him. The American Revolution had given the country political freedom from Great Britain. Americans were eager to create a distinct national identity for the new republic. Writers in the United States began to use Americans and American events for the subjects of their books, songs, and plays. Crockett stepped onto the national scene at just the right time. Who was a better representative of a true American than David Crockett?

A Crockett-like character soon was gracing the stage in a play by James K. Paulding that was first performed in New York City. The play, which debuted in 1831, was called *The Lion of the West*. Its main character was a frontier politician named Colonel Nimrod Wildfire. Pitted against a variety of eastern and foreign characters, Wildfire overcame them all with his humor and frontier intellect. It was clear to everyone that Nimrod Wildfire was David Crockett. Instead of being angry about the imitation, Crockett was thrilled to be portrayed as the play's

This portrait of James K. Paulding (1778–1860) is by A. S. Conrad. Paulding pushed for the development of an original, creative American culture, which was not dependent on that of England. Paulding, a writer, also served as a U.S. Navy agent in New York City and in 1838, was appointed secretary of the navy.

hero. He even accepted an invitation to attend the show in Washington in 1831. The actor playing Wildfire knew David Crockett was in the audience. He bowed and waved at the congressman, who bowed and waved back. The crowd roared with approval as the two men saluted each other.

Crockett was much less pleased with another work in which he appeared. Published in 1833, *Life and Adventures of Colonel David Crockett of West Tennessee* was a collection of stories about him. The

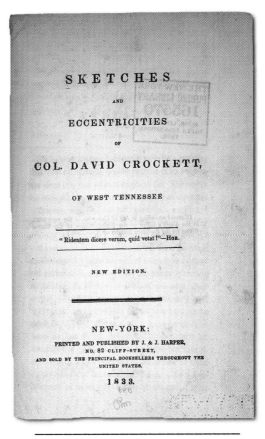

Sketches and Eccentricities of Col. David Crockett, of West Tennessee, not written by Crockett, made him write his own book to correct the misleading stories in this one.

book was reprinted in the same year under the title *Sketches and Eccentricities of Col. David Crockett, of West Tennessee*. The author claimed he had spoken to people who knew Crockett and had even visited the frontiersman at his Tennessee home. Crockett objected to the biography, because he said parts of it were untrue. He did not receive any money from the book, even though it was written about him and used his real name.

MR. FRANK MAYO, AS "DAVY CROCKETT."

SARONY, 680 BROADWAY, N. Y.

Boston-born Frank Mayo starred in the title role of *Davy Crockett;
or, Be Sure You're Right, Then Go Ahead*, an 1872 play by Frank
Murdoch. This is Mayo's *carte de visite*, or calling card, which is a small
portrait that used to be sold or distributed for income or publicity.

Crockett's solution was to write his autobiography. Who better could tell of his rise from poverty to the halls of Congress? Although he had fought Native Americans and had hunted bears, Crockett had never written a book. He asked friend and fellow congressman Thomas Chilton of Kentucky for help. Chilton took Crockett's rough draft and readied it for publication. It was titled *A Narrative of the Life of David Crockett of the State of Tennessee.* Appearing for sale in 1834, the book contained many stories that Crockett had used while campaigning for office. His frontier grammar amused readers, who enjoyed its authentic style. The book introduced his motto to the public, "Be always sure you're right—THEN GO AHEAD." In 1835, there appeared the first of many almanacs based on his adventures. With so much attention focused on Crockett from the play, the unauthorized biography and his autobiography, and newspapers, his name was soon on the lips of many Americans.

Not everyone was pleased with Crockett's growing fame. The president was especially displeased. Always independent, since 1834 Crockett had begun to fight with his old commander, Andrew Jackson. The president and his supporters expected each member of the Democratic party, including Crockett, to vote for the laws that Jackson wanted passed.

Crockett disagreed with some of Jackson's ideas and spoke out against him. Jackson became very angry at Crockett and swore to block his reelection to Congress.

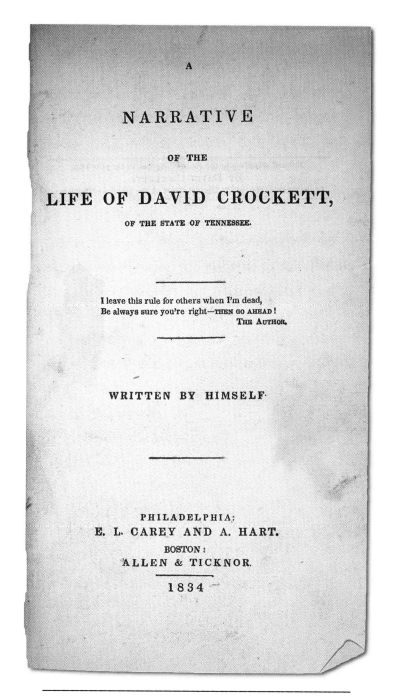

In 1834, David Crockett published his autobiography,
A Narrative of the Life of David Crockett of the State of Tennessee.
In this book, Crockett described his earliest days in Tennessee,
his two marriages, his bear hunts, and also his political activities.

"Crockett on President Jackson"
from *An Account of Col. Crockett's Tour to the
North and Down East*

I voted for Andrew Jackson because
I believed he possessed certain principles,
and not because his name was
Andrew Jackson, or the Hero, or
Old Hickory. And when he left those
principles which induced me to support him,
I considered myself justified in opposing
him. This thing of man-worship I am a
stranger to; I don't like it; it taints every
action of life; it is like a skunk getting
into a house—long after he has cleared out,
you smell him in every room and closet,
from the cellar to the garret.

Jackson also had political opponents who wanted him out of office. They claimed that Jackson acted more like a king than a president and nicknamed him King Andrew. They called themselves Whigs, because that was the name of the party that opposed the king in Great Britain. Whig leaders began to see Crockett, who had gained a national following, as a possible candidate for their party in the next presidential election.

Crockett claimed that he still held the same ideas he'd had when he was elected to Congress. He said that Jackson, not he, had been the one to change. Friends warned Crockett that he was heading into trouble and that the Whigs were not to be trusted. He had become convinced, however, that he could become president. After all, he had started out as a poor frontiersman and was now a popular celebrity. The title of President Crockett had a ring to it that he liked. He accompanied Whig leaders on a three-week tour of the New England states. At each stop he told his humorous stories and spoke out against Jackson. Two more books appeared under Crockett's name, which were little more than political attacks on Jackson and his party. The Whigs delighted in Crockett's performances. The president and his supporters became even more angry at Crockett's betrayal of their party.

The Gentleman from the Cane returned home in the summer of 1835 to campaign for reelection to the House of Representatives. He found that Jackson's supporters

This political cartoon, drawn during Andrew Jackson's presidency, depicts Jackson as an absolute monarch who abuses his veto power and tramples on the Constitution. The cartoon was created between 1828 and 1836.

*The Whig party
was formally organized in
1834. It consisted of several groups
united mainly by their dislike of President
Andrew Jackson and what was seen as
his excessive power. The party borrowed
the name Whig from the British party
opposed to royal prerogatives. The two
great leaders of the Whig party
were Henry Clay and
Daniel Webster.*

in Tennessee planned to do all they could to keep him from winning his old seat. Crockett was not worried at first and believed that most voters approved of his behavior. However, many remained loyal to General Jackson because of his status as a war hero, and they disapproved of Crockett's attack on him. Others disagreed with Crockett's stand on certain issues. He faced the charge that activities such as writing books and touring New England kept him from representing the voters who had elected him. They wondered if he cared more about his political future than he did about them. Crockett answered all the charges in his typical way.

This is a portrayal of the 1836 presidential election contest as a horse race between the four candidates. The print, published by H. R. Robinson, probably appeared when hopes for a Whig nomination were still considered realistic.

This time, however, his speeches and stories failed him. He ran a close campaign to return to the House of Representatives, but his opponent, a Jackson man named Adam Huntsman, won by a narrow margin of about 250 votes.

8. Texas Calls

Crockett would not be going back to Congress. He had lost elections before, but this time it was different. His defeat ended any Whig interest in his candidacy for president. How could he be expected to win a national election if he could not even win his district? Crockett, who had rejected his own party, now had no party at all to support him. Without party support, there was no political future.

Nevertheless, former congressman Crockett had been in politics long enough to know that things could change. Although he was out of favor now, there were always other elections. What he needed to do was put his defeat behind him. In the frontier tradition, he knew it was time to move on once again.

Crockett had stated in his attacks on Jackson that if the president and his supporters kept control of the government, then he would move to Texas rather than stay in the same county with them. It was time now to make good on his promise. He had not said that he would stay in Texas permanently, so he could always

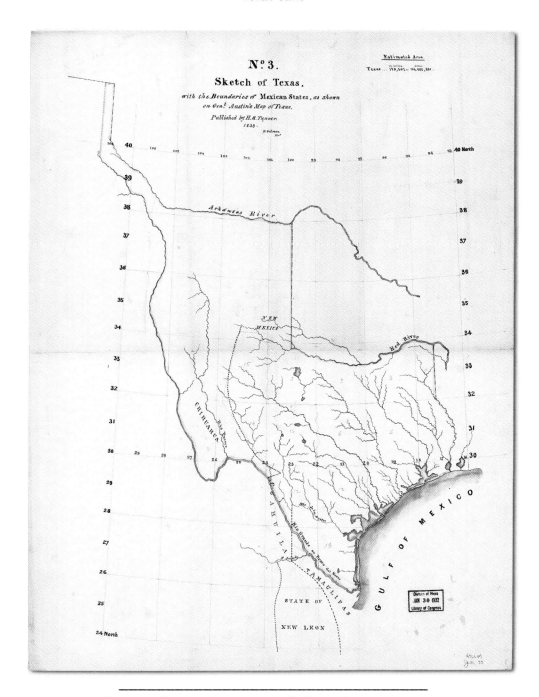

This is a sketch of Texas with the boundaries of Mexican states as shown on General Stephen F. Austin's map of Texas published by R. S. Tanner in 1839. After David Crockett's political career stalled in Tennessee, he saw Texas as a new horizon with a new government where he could flourish.

return to the United States if he wanted. On the brighter side, the trip would be a chance to hunt again, something he had missed during his years in Washington. In November 1835, David Crockett set out for Texas with a small band of relatives and friends on what would be his last and greatest adventure.

Texas was Mexican territory in 1835. Mexico had won its independence from Spain in 1821, after a revolution that had lasted ten years. Thus the Republic of Mexico and the United States both owed their existence to having broken away from European kings. The two nations also shared the same debate over which should have more power: the individual states that make up the nation or the national government. In 1824, the Mexican congress adopted a constitution that organized Mexico into a federal republic. In Mexico, supporters of strong state government were called Federalists. The supporters of a strong national government in Mexico were called Centralists.

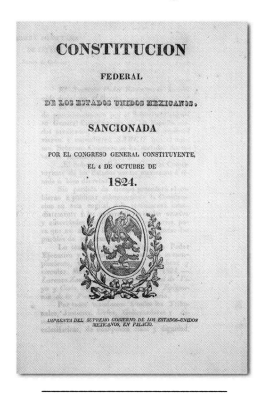

The Mexican constitution of 1824 provided for a federal republic and set various goals, toward which the nation slowly inched its way.

By autumn 1835, when Crockett decided to go to Texas, Mexico had erupted into a civil war between the Federalists and the Centralists.

In 1833, a Mexican general named Antonio López de Santa Anna was elected president. He had told voters that he was a Federalist, but after a year in office he announced that he had become a Centralist. He had his supporters in the Mexican congress throw out the federal constitution of 1824. State governments were also abolished. These actions upset several of the Mexican states. Soon northern Mexico was in revolt against Santa Anna and the Centralist government.

Mexico's self-proclaimed dictator Santa Anna led Mexican forces against the Texan revolt of 1835–1836, first winning at the Battle of the Alamo before being defeated and captured.

Texas was part of the Mexican state called Coahuila y Tejas. Spain had had a problem attracting settlers to Texas, because it was a wilderness controlled by roaming bands of Native Americans. Mexico inherited this problem when it became independent. Mexican officials decided to invite citizens from the United States and Europe to settle in Texas after attempts to inhabit the region with Mexicans failed. Bringing settlers to Texas would provide a barrier between Mexico and the warlike Native Americans to the north. It would also stimulate Mexico's economy. Many Americans were eager for land, even if it meant moving to another country. The settlement was to be conducted by contractors called empresarios, who would recruit those people willing to come. The plan worked too well. By 1829, in some parts of Texas, Anglo Texans, who called themselves Texans, outnumbered Mexican Texans, called Tejanos, by ten to one. The Mexican government, fearing that Texas was becoming more American than Mexican, changed its policy in an effort to gain control of the colonists.

Americans who settled in Texas were required to become Mexican citizens and to obey Mexican laws. Although they changed their citizenship, they did not forget the lessons of the American Revolution. They began to make comparisons between events in 1776 and those that they were witnessing. The British government had raised taxes, abolished legislatures, sent troops to occupy their towns, seized weapons, and arrested its citizens. The Mexican government was now engaged in the exact same activities. The Texans revolted, as had their parents and grandparents before them. The Tejanos faced a hard decision: should they join the revolt or remain loyal to the national government? Many were opposed to the Centralists and sided with the Texans.

Crockett knew of the trouble in Texas even before he set out on his journey. He had told people that he was going there to hunt, and hunt he did. Texas pleased him because game was plentiful and the soil was rich. He hunted buffalo, an animal that no longer could be found east of the Mississippi River. He saw many bees swarming near trees and knew that where there was honey, bears would not be far away. Although he may have come on a hunting trip, Crockett wrote home that he was ready to settle in Texas, telling his children that it was the "garden spot of the world." He further explained, "I am in hopes of making a fortune yet for myself and my family bad as my prospect has been." The fact that Texas was in revolt did not seem to worry him. At age 49, Crockett had started out on his last and greatest adventure.

9. The Fight Against Santa Anna

David Crockett enlisted as a volunteer in the Texas army, agreeing to serve for six months. The Texans were delighted to have Crockett join them in their fight against Santa Anna and the Centralists. His skill with a rifle was well known, and they welcomed his help. Parties and dinners were held in his honor, and he was always called on to make a speech. Colonel Crockett would laugh and say that he had come to serve as a "high private," meaning that he wanted no special treatment. Crockett told his family that he would rather be in his present situation than be elected to the U.S. Congress for life. He tried to downplay the danger, writing, "Do not be uneasy about me. I am with my friends."

Crockett had reason to be hopeful about his future. There was the promise of the land he would receive for serving as a soldier. In addition, the Texans were forming a new government, and Crockett expected to be elected to the convention that would write its constitutions. He lost the election but was not worried. There would be other elections once Texas won its independence. His experience in the Tennessee legislature and in the House of Representatives certainly gave him an advantage in any future race. For now, however, political battles took a backseat to the real fighting that was to be done.

Crockett and the men he had been traveling with were sent to San Antonio. He did not ride directly there but took time to hunt and to explore. On February 7, 1836, Crockett and his friends entered the old Spanish town and reported to the Texan commander, Lieutenant Colonel James C. Neill. The Tennesseans were assigned quarters in town. Soon word spread of Crockett's arrival, and the typical rounds of parties, dinners, and speeches followed for the next few weeks. Crockett repeated his reason for coming to Texas and pledged to defend it from Santa Anna and the Centralists.

San Antonio was the most important town in Texas. Only a few months before, it had been controlled by Centralist soldiers. In December, however, Texan soldiers aided by volunteers from the United States attacked and captured the Mexican garrison. The defeated Mexican army withdrew from Texas after promising not to fight the Texans again. Santa Anna, however, was determined to retake San Antonio and to crush the rebels. He gathered his troops, including those driven out of Texas, and marched northward. He split his force and sent one part to Goliad, a town southeast of San Antonio. Santa Anna and the rest of the army headed for San Antonio.

Santa Anna arrived outside San Antonio on February 23, 1836. The Texans knew that he was coming but had not expected him so soon. Learning of his approach, troops that had not already done so withdrew to an old mission across the river from the town. The mission, used for many years by the Spanish and the Mexicans as a military barracks, had been turned into a fort during the previous battle for San Antonio. The old fortified mission was called the Alamo.

The Texans had two new commanders. Colonel Neill had departed from San Antonio in mid-February on a leave of absence to check on his wife and children, who

This 1847 painting of the Alamo church is by
Edward Everett. Everett was a soldier stationed in
San Antonio, Texas, during the Mexican-American War.

were ill, and to arrange for more supplies and men for his post. Before departing, he turned over his command to William B. Travis, an officer in the regular Texas army. Many of the volunteers did not want to serve under a regular officer, and they elected James Bowie as their leader. The two men agreed to share command as a way of preserving harmony among the garrison. Crockett, still acting as a "high private," entered the Alamo and offered to serve wherever he was needed. Travis assigned him and his fellow Tennesseans the task of defending a low wooden wall, called a palisade. They took their places and stood ready to beat back any attackers.

Santa Anna and his army arrived in San Antonio on February 23, 1836. They began a siege of the Alamo that lasted for thirteen days. On the second day of the siege, Colonel Bowie grew ill, and Colonel Travis became the Alamo's sole commander. He had only about 150 men, while Santa Anna had several thousand. Travis wrote a series of letters asking for help and sent them out by messengers. The letters, directed to the temporary government, vividly explained the danger faced by the men inside the Alamo. One group of thirty-two men from the town of Gonzales answered his call for help and marched into the fort early on the

Next spread: David Crockett swings an empty rifle at enemy soldiers in Robert Onderdonk's painting entitled *Fall of the Alamo*. During the Battle of the Alamo, all the Texan defenders were killed. Losses in the battle have been placed at 189 Texans against about 1,600 Mexicans.

morning of March 1, having sneaked through Santa Anna's lines. Although other Texans attempted to reach San Antonio, they were unable to arrive in time. Early on the morning of March 6, 1836, Santa Anna ordered his soldiers to attack the Alamo. Shortly after the sun came up, the Alamo was captured and the entire Texan garrison was killed, including Colonel Crockett.

Santa Anna's attack had overwhelmed the men inside the Alamo. The assault had been launched just before dawn, when most of the garrison had been resting. Rushing to defend the walls, the Texans found Mexican troops approaching the fort from four directions. The Texans were outnumbered by at least ten to one. Thick clouds of smoke from burning gunpowder filled the air and made it difficult to see what was happening beyond a few yards. Despite initial success in fending off the attack, the Texans were driven from the walls, an event that forced many to seek cover in the numerous rooms that ringed the perimeter of the compound. The desperate battle finally came to an end once the Mexican soldiers used the Texans' own cannons, abandoned when they fell back, to fire round after round into the buildings that sheltered the remaining defenders. The last of the fighting most likely pitted Mexican bayonets against Texan bowie knives, a very brutal and personal type of combat.

David Crockett's activities during the siege and battle remain somewhat of a mystery. Based on his previous exploits, it is easy to imagine that he played a major role in the Alamo's defense. Travis praised him in one of his messages, saying "The Hon. David Crockett was seen at all points, animating the men to do their duty." Texans throughout Texas were glad that Crockett was there to help in its defense. Wrote one volunteer at Goliad to his mother, "The Mexicans have made two successive attacks on the Alamo in which the gallant little garrison repulsed them with some loss. Probably David Crockett 'grinned' them off." Crockett, a natural leader, amused the garrison with his stories to keep up their spirits. He also brought his fiddle and played for them. His skill with the rifle must have been especially welcomed. Travis and other members of the garrison must have felt better just having the famous frontiers-man with them.

With so much public interest in his life, there is also interest in his death. Many people like to think that he fought like a lion until he was overcome. Several Mexican soldiers describe another end for him. These witnesses claim that Crockett and a few others survived the battle only to be captured when the fighting stopped. Bloodied and exhausted, they were taken to Santa Anna. Instead of sparing Crockett and his companions, Santa Anna ordered them to be executed. According to this account, with his body beaten but his spirit unbroken, David Crockett bravely accepted his fate.

This engraving shows David Crockett dying in battle at the Alamo. He died a hero's death, at age 49. Although the battle at the Alamo did little to halt Santa Anna and the huge Mexican army physically, the Texans' bloody defeat stirred a cry for revenge that would later help to topple Santa Anna's forces.

People in Texas and the United States were stunned to learn that Crockett had been killed in such a ruthless manner. His death and the slaying of the Alamo garrison would have a great effect on the revolution that would result in Texas's independence. Santa Anna's soldiers had also captured the Texan garrison at Goliad and had put more than 300 soldiers to death. Travis had warned that the revolution would end in either "Victory or Death!" The killing of so many of their friends and countrymen caused volunteers to join the Texan forces. Santa Anna had to be stopped, or all the Texans and Tejanos who supported the revolution would be either killed or driven out of Texas.

G · WILLIAM IRVINE LEWIS · WILLIAM J. LIGHTFOOT
AM MILLS · ISAAC MILLSAPS · EDWARD F. MITCHA
ILLO · WILLIAM PARKS · RICHARDSON PERRY ·

David Crockett appears at the center of this marble monument that was built at the Alamo. Crockett stands for the spirit of the American frontier. He became a legend of the Old West within his lifetime, and his popularity continues to this day.

The Texans reorganized their forces after the defeats in San Antonio and Goliad and vowed to fight Santa Anna. On the afternoon of April 21, 1836, Santa Anna and an advance wing of his army were resting on the banks of the San Jacinto River, near the site of present-day Houston, Texas. Approximately 900 Texans attacked and quickly overcame the Centralists, killing 630 and capturing another 730. Nine Texans were killed and only thirty were wounded. As they attacked, the Texans cried out, "Remember the Alamo!" and "Remember Goliad!" Perhaps thought but unsaid were the words "Remember David Crockett."

10. Crockett's Legacy

Although Crockett died in 1836, his legend lived on and even grew. The *Davy Crockett Almanack* continued to be published for years after his fall at the Alamo. One edition explained that he had left stories with the publishers before going to Texas, an explanation that readers did not really believe. However, they did not care. Americans had a hunger to know more about their hero, even if stories about him often strayed from the truth. Throughout the 1800s, Crockett remained the subject of plays, books, and songs.

Storytellers took advantage of new ways to portray Crockett once the twentieth century dawned. In addition to books and live performances by actors, movies kept Crockett's memory alive. The first movie based on Crockett appeared in 1909. Many others followed, the most famous of which has been John Wayne's 1960 film entitled *The Alamo*.

Crockett also came directly into people's homes through the invention of television. In 1955, when television was still new, Walt Disney produced a series of

one-hour episodes about Crockett that aired on Disney's popular Sunday-evening program. The series had a catchy theme song that soon had the nation singing the refrain, "Davy, Davy Crockett, king of the wild frontier." Frontiersman, soldier, congressman, and hero, David Crockett is truly a frontier legend who will be remembered for generations to come.

Opposite: John Wayne played the character of David Crockett in the 1960 film *The Alamo*, which Wayne also directed. For this film, Wayne's production crew reconstructed the Alamo mission in Bracketville, Texas, several hundred miles (km) from the actual site of the Alamo.

Timeline

1786	David Crockett is born on August 17 in Greene County, Tennessee.
1798	Twelve-year-old Crockett is hired out to Jacob Siler of Virginia.
1799	Crockett runs away from Siler and returns home. A fight at school causes him to run away from home.
1802	Crockett returns home and makes up with his father.
1806	Mary Finley (Polly) marries Crockett on August 16.
1811	Polly, David, and their two sons move to Lincoln County, Tennessee.
1813	Crockett serves as a scout in the Tennessee militia during the Creek War.
1815	The end of the war allows Crockett to return home.
	Mary has a daughter but dies.
1816	Crockett marries a local widow, Elizabeth

Patton, who has two children of her own.

1817   Crockett moves his family to Lawrence County, Tennessee.

1821   Voters elect Crockett to the Tennessee legislature.

1822   Crockett explores newly open lands in western Tennessee.

He moves his family to western Tennessee.

1826   An attempt to sell a cargo of barrel staves ends in failure when Crockett's two flatboats sink in the Mississippi River near Memphis, Tennessee.

1827   Crockett is elected to the House of Representatives.

1828   Crockett's former Army commander, Andrew Jackson, is elected president.

1831   The play *The Lion of the West* opens, featuring a main character named Nimrod Wildfire, who is based on David Crockett.

1833   Sale of a book entitled *Sketches and Eccentricities of Col. David Crockett, of West Tennessee* increases Crockett's popularity with the American public.

Crockett wins back his seat in the House of Representatives.

1834 Crockett publishes his autobiography, *A Narrative of the Life of David Crockett of the State of Tennessee.*

His opposition to Jackson makes him attractive as a possible presidential candidate for the Whig party.

1835 Angered by his continued split with Andrew Jackson, voters choose not to return Crockett to the House of Representatives. He leaves for Texas.

1836 Crockett enlists as a volunteer in the revolt against Mexico and vows to support any republican-style government that may be formed in the future.

He is killed at the Battle of the Alamo on March 6, 1836.

Glossary

almanac (AHL-muh-nak) A book containing information about the weather that also usually has other useful information and humorous stories.

Anglo (ANG-gloh) A person of English descent.

aristocrats (uh-RIS-tuh-krats) People who are born into a high social position.

backcountry (BAK-kun-tree) The area beyond the established line of settlements; also called frontier.

barracks (BAR-iks) The building in which soldiers live.

bayonets (BAY-oh-nets) Knives attached to the front ends of rifles.

bottomland (BAH-tum-land) The flat land along a creek or a stream that is rich but that often floods.

bowie knife (BOO-ee NYF) A kind of hunting knife.

cane (KAYN) A tall, bamboolike plant that grows along creek banks and the edges of swamps.

civil (SIH-vul) The portion of government usually run by elected officials.

commerce (KAH-mers) Business, such as the buying and selling of goods.

crack shot (KRAK SHOT) An expert shot with a firearm, also known as a marksman.

creditor (KREH-dih-tur) A person to whom money is owed.

Declaration of Independence (deh-kluh-RAY-shun UV in-duh-PEN-dints) The document signed in 1776, in which Americans explained their ideas about government and announced that they were breaking away from Great Britain.

democratic (deh-muh-KRAH-tik) A form of government in which members help make decisions, usually by casting votes.

district (DIS-trikt) A political division of land intended to help organize government within its boundaries.

factions (FAK-shunz) A group of people who share opinions and support the same policies.

federal republic (FEH-drul ree-PUB-lik) A political arrangement in which states agree to form a national government to cooperate on matters of common interest. However, the states keep most of their power to control matters with their own borders.

freight (FRAYT) Goods carried by wagon or boat to either a merchant or a customer.

frontier (frun-TEER) The area beyond the established line of settlements; also called backcountry.

game (GAYM) Wild animals that are hunted for food.

garret (GAR-uht) An attic or top room of a house.

garrison (GAR-ih-son) A group of soldiers assigned to guard a town or a fort.

junction (JUNK-shun) The place where one river flows into another.

marksmanship (MARKS-mun-ship) Being an expert shot with a firearm, also known as a crack shot.

migration (my-GRAY-shun) The mass movement of people or animals from one place to another.

mill (MIL) A building that houses machinery for grinding grain, sawing logs, or other types of work.

mission (MIH-shun) A complex consisting of dormitories, workshops, and a church, built by the Spanish to convert Native Americans into Spanish subjects.

Quaker (KWAY-kur) A member of a religious group known as the Society of Friends. Quakers were opposed to war.

porticoes (POR-tih-kohz) Porches that usually have columns supporting the roof.

powder horn (POW-der HORN) A waterproof container made from a bull's horn that held gunpowder.

Protestants (PRAH-tihs-tunts) People who formed a separate branch of Christianity as an alternative to Catholicism, or the Catholic Church.

republic (rih-PUB-lik) A form of government in which members, usually called citizens, elect representatives to make laws for them.

shucking bee (SHUHK-ing BEE) A party where people hold contests to see who can peel the leaves off ears of corn the fastest.

squatter (SKWAH-ter) A person who settles on land that he or she does not own.

squaw (SKWAH) A Native American woman.

truant (TROO-int) Absent or missing from an assigned place or task.

Union (YOON-yun) Another name for the United States that refers to the joining or uniting of the various states into one nation.

U.S. Constitution (YOO ES kahn-stih-TOO-shun) The document adopted in 1789 that explains the different parts of the nation's government and how each works.

Whigs (WIGZ) A political party formed of people who opposed President Andrew Jackson and his policies.

Additional Resources

To learn more about David Crockett, check out these books and Web sites:

Books

Parks, Aileen Wells. *Davy Crockett: Young Rifleman (Childhood of Famous American Series)*. New York: Simon & Schuster Children's, 1983.

Santrey, Laurence. *Davy Crockett: Young Pioneer*. Mahwah, New Jersey: Troll Communications L.L.C., 1990.

Townsend, Tom. *Davy Crockett: An American Hero*. Austin, Texas: Eakin Press, 1993.

Web Sites

Due to the changing nature of Internet links, PowerPlus Books has developed an online list of Web sites related to the subject of this book. This site is updated regularly. Please use this link to access the list:

www.powerkidslinks.com/lalt/crockett/

Bibliography

Anonymous. *Sketches and Eccentricities of Col. David Crockett, of West Tennessee*. New York: Harper and Brothers, Publishers, 1833.

Crockett, David. *An Account of Col. Crockett's Tour to the North and Down East*. Philadelphia, Pennsylvania: Carey and Hart, 1835.

Crockett, Davy. *A Narrative of the Life of Davy Crockett, Written by Himself*. Philadelphia, Pennsylvania: Carey and Hart, 1834.

Crutchfield, Jim, ed. *Davy Crockett's Almanacks, 1835–1843*. Union City, Tennessee: Pioneer Press, 1986.

Huffines, Alan and Gary Zaboly. *The Blood of Noble Men: The Alamo Siege and Battle*. Austin, Texas: Eakin Press, 1999.

Lofaro, Michael A. and Joe Cummings, eds. *Crockett at Two Hundred: New Perspectives on the Man and the Myth*. Knoxville, Tennessee: University of Tennessee Press, 1989.

Shackford, James A. *David Crockett: The Man and the Legend*. Chapel Hill, North Carolina: University of North Carolina Press, 1956.

Index

About the Author

Richard Bruce Winders is a recognized authority on U.S.-Mexican relations during the first half of the nineteenth century. *Mr. Polk's Army: The American Military Experience in the Mexican War* received the Jerry Coffey Memorial Book Prize for the best work in the field of military history for 1997. Winders served as assistant editor on *The United States and Mexico at War: Nineteenth-Century Expansionism and Conflict*, an encyclopedia project for Macmillan (1998). He has developed educational programs and material designed to assist teachers and students. A study entitled *Crisis in the Southwest: The United States and Mexico and the Struggle Over Texas* is scheduled for release in spring 2002. Awarded his doctorate in U.S. history from Texas Christian University, Winders has held the position of historian/curator at the Alamo since 1996.

Credits

Photo Credits

Cover: National Portrait Gallery, Smithsonian Institution, future bequest of Ms. Katharine Bradford (portrait); H.A.McArdle ("Dawn at the Alamo"); pp. 4, 6 National Portrait Gallery, Smithsonian Institution / Art Resource, New York; pp. 8, 39 Tennessee Historical Society; p. 9 National Archives and Records Administration; pp. 10, 11, 25, 35, 43, 46, 67, 81 Library of Congress, Geography and Map Division, Washington, D.C.; p. 13 Historic American Buildings Survey, Library of Congress, Prints and Photograph Division; pp. 14, 15 Tennessee State Library and Archives, Archives and Manuscript Collections; p. 17 Tennessee State Museum Exhibits; pp. 18, 52, 53 Lawrence County Archives, Lawrenceburg, Tennessee; p. 20 © Lee Snider; Lee Snider/CORBIS; p. 24 courtesy of the Saint Louis Art Museum; p. 26 reproduced with permission from the Robert H. Gore, Jr. Numismatic Collection, Department of Special Collections, University of Notre Dame Libraries; p. 28 Jefferson County Archives, Dandridge, Tennessee; p. 30 Dover Pictorial Archive; p. 31 (top) © Buddy Mays/CORBIS; p. 31 (bottom) David Crockett's Rifle, Gift of Mr. and Mrs. Paul L. Failor, The Alamo Collection, photograph courtesy of the Daughters of the Republic of Texas Library; p. 32 Tennessee State Museum, Tennessee Historical Society Collection; p. 33 National Museum of American History, S. I.; pp. 36, 62, 64–65 the Phelps Stokes Collection, Miriam and Ira D. Wallach Division of Art, Prints, and Photographs, New York Public Library, Astor, Lenox and Tilden Foundations; pp. 38, 54, 77 © Bettmann/CORBIS; p. 49 Chicago Historical Society; pp. 55, 94 © CORBIS; p. 56 Independence National Historical Park; pp. 58, 60, 79 Library of Congress Prints and Photographs Division; p. 70 courtesy of the Navy Art Collection, Washington, D.C.; p. 71, 74 General Research Division, New York Public Library, Astor, Lenox and Tilden Foundations; p. 72 The New York Public Library for the Performing Arts, Billy Rose Theatre Collection, J. H. James Collection; p. 82 Tarlton Law Library, University of Texas School of Law; p. 83 the San Jacinto Museum of History, Houston, Texas; p. 88 Amon Carter Museum, Fort Worth, Texas, Gift Mrs. Anne Burnett Tandy in memory of her father Thomas Loyd Burnett, 1870–1938; pp. 90-91 Friends of the Governor's Mansion, Austin, Texas; p. 95 Maura Boruchow; p. 98 Movie Still Archives.

Editor Leslie Kaplan

Series Design Laura Murawski

Layout Design Corinne Jacob

Photo Researcher Jeffrey Wendt